the Nurdge in my Side

2007-8 NMI
MISSION EDUCATION RESOURCES

❋ ❋ ❋

BOOKS

AFRICA'S SOUL HOPE
The AIDS Crisis and the Church
by Ellen Decker

BABOONS ON THE RUNWAY
And Other Humorous Stories from Africa
by Richard F. Zanner

MEETING JESUS
by Keith Schwanz

THE NUDGE IN MY SIDE
Stories from Indonesia and the Philippines
by The Bob McCroskeys

THEY SAW ONLY FEET
More Life Lessons from Missionary Kids
by Dean Nelson

A LOVE STORY FROM TRINIDAD
by Ruth O. Saxon

❋ ❋ ❋

ADULT MISSION EDUCATION RESOURCE BOOK

RESPONDING TO MISSION CHALLENGES
Editors: Aimee Curtis and Rosanne Bolerjack

the Nudge in my Side

STORIES FROM INDONESIA AND THE PHILIPPINES

by
The Bob McCroskeys

Nazarene Publishing House
Kansas City, Missouri

Copyright 2007
Nazarene Publishing House

ISBN-13: 978-0-8341-2291-8
ISBN-10: 0-8341-2291-X

Printed in the United States of America

Editor: Aimee Curtis
Cover Design: Brandon Hill
Interior Design: Sharon Page

10 9 8 7 6 5 4 3 2 1

Contents

Acknowledgments		8
Introduction		9
1	James Wambrauw—Indonesia	11
2	Pepi Causing—Philippines	22
3	Yez—Indonesia	32
4	Eva—Philippines	43
5	Pak Karjan—Indonesia	52
6	Juanito and Hannah—Philippines	63
Epilogue		73
Call to Action		75
Pronunciation Guide		77

The Bob McCroskeys Sr. and Jr. have spent much of their lives in the more than 21,000 islands of the Republic of the Philippines and Indonesia serving as missionaries for the Church of the Nazarene.

Bob Sr. and Tillie McCroskey arrived in the Philippines in 1956 and retired in 1990 after 34 years of service. Following retirement, they were called back to coordinate the first Asia-Pacific regional convention held in Manila. They were assigned to the regional office and spent a year preparing for and directing this event. Following this they were assigned to Hong Kong for a year to replace furloughing missionaries. Their ministry was primarily in field evangelism and administration. Bob was mission director for many of those years.

Bob Jr. and Rosa McCroskey arrived in Indonesia in 1975 and have served as missionaries for over 30 years. Their ministry has been in education and administration. Bob was founder and first rector of the Indonesia Nazarene Theological College where both he and Rosa are still teaching full-time. He has served first as mission director and then field director of the Sealands (South East Asia Islands) field for the last 20 years.

Acknowledgments

We have many people we would like to thank for making this book possible.

First, we are grateful for the collegial relationships with our coworkers in our areas of responsibility. We have been fellow laborers together, and certainly without them and their stories this book would not have been possible.

Second, we are grateful to our families for their support. We have always felt that being a missionary was a calling that extended to every member of the family. We have all had a part in ministering together. This book reflects that. It is a three-generation endeavor. Bob Sr. and Bob Jr. wrote the stories, and granddaughter/daughter Kara helped with editing.

Finally, we are grateful to the Church of the Nazarene for recognizing God's call in our lives and committing the resources and support to make it possible for us to answer that call. We recognize that many of you have had a great investment in our lives. Our two families represent a combined total of 207 missionary years in our respective countries. Thank you for enabling us to serve the Lord as Nazarene missionaries.

Introduction

We planted a church in a small mountain village outside the city of Yogyakarta in Indonesia ("Yogya" for short). Coconut Mountain is a community of simple and poor farmers. The area is known all over the island of Java because of its extensive poverty due to minimal rainfall and consequent water and crop difficulties.

When we began work in this area, the gospel was as unheard of as free parking in New York City. But as God helped us plant and water the seed, He also enabled us to reap an abundant harvest of souls that resulted in a strong church. Then began the task of discipling these converts to understand what it meant to be a Christian as well as a Nazarene.

In one particular evening service, we explained what testimonies were and gave an opportunity for these new Christians to share how God was working in their lives. It was a little slow starting at first, but once the ice was broken we had a steady stream of speakers—the next one standing up as soon as the previous one sat down. It was exciting! Then came a lull, and as we looked out across the group we noticed an older man lean over and nudge a younger man in the side with his elbow. Then he whispered something in the young man's ear. After a while the young man stood up and spoke—only it wasn't his testimony. Instead, he explained, it was the testimony of the older man sitting next to him. Perhaps the older man felt unsure of speaking in public, or perhaps he was conversant only in his tribal language and not the national language. We'll never know. But what we learned was that the old man felt God's presence and faithfulness so intensely it was burning in his heart. And no language barrier could put out that flame. So he nudged his neighbor to be the one to speak on his behalf.

In that same spirit, we want to share testimonies of some of our friends with you. We have felt the nudge in our side too. Our friends are not able to tell you their stories themselves as they also have language barriers to hurdle. But they have thrilling testimonies of God's presence and faithfulness in their lives, and they would like us to share those with you.

So pull up a chair. Open your hearts. Let us tell you their stories.

The Bob McCroskeys

"Therefore go and make disciples of all nations"
(Matt. 28:19*a*).

James Wambrauw
INDONESIA

Everyone knew Insan Brasi. He was a leader in his village on the island of Biak in the province of Irian Jaya/Papua. He was also a headhunter, and he and his fellow villagers were cannibals. A giant of a man, he stood head and shoulders taller than most of his tribe. When his village waged war against one of the surrounding villages, Insan Brasi was always in the lead. His machete was so heavy that most men had trouble lifting it. But Insan Brasi wielded it with ease. When he led his village into battle, they never lost. Insan always sought out the leader on the opposing side and killed him. He would then march his villagers back in triumphal procession carrying with him his personal trophy of victory: his enemy's head. He even had a small room where he kept all of these heads as permanent proof of his great fighting prowess.

Insan Brasi was famous. Most who knew him hated him. Hardly a surrounding village was left untouched by the grief of death because of him. He had many enemies who wanted him dead. But Insan was always on alert. Even at night he brought his killing machete to bed with him. He had a special pillow made, a small wooden box with a hole cut out in the middle for his ear, and he was ever attuned to even the most stealthy approach of an enemy in the middle of the night. While his enemies hated him, they feared him even more. They knew if any of them was brave enough to fight against Insan Brasi, surely his own life would be forfeited. But his enemies met together often to come up with a plan to destroy him. Finally they devised a scheme they thought might work. Insan Brasi had a younger brother who was also a giant of a man. These enemies approached this brother and offered him a staggering sum of money if he would kill Insan for them. Normally, of course, a brother would not consider killing a member of his own family, but the reward was so great he said he would do it.

Insan's brother knew he would have to lay his plans carefully and succeed the first time. He would not live for a second attempt. One day as Insan Brasi came in from a hard day in the fields, his brother met him with a delicious coconut milk drink. The milk was still in its original container—a large green coconut that took two hands to lift. As Insan brought the coconut to his mouth, he exposed his rib cage— the instant his brother was waiting for. His brother grabbed his machete and swung hard. At the last second, Insan sensed the treachery and lowered his elbow to parry the blow. Still it opened up a deep gash in his side.

Letting out a mighty bellow of rage, Insan grabbed his own machete and began to fight his brother. Fellow villagers crouched in terror as these two giants fought each other. In the end, Insan made one final strike and killed his treacherous brother before he, too, fell over dead from his wounds.

Suddenly the two great protectors of the Brasi clan were gone. The surrounding villagers met gleefully to make plans for revenge killings. The remaining members of the Brasi clan knew that staying in their village meant certain death, so they scattered.

One of the sons who fled was named Yohan. He eventually ended up in the provincial capital city of Jayapura where he met a girl fleeing a similar background as his. They soon married and began to raise a family. One of their sons was named James. When James graduated from high school, he obtained permission from his parents to attend university on the main island of Java. He boarded a boat bound for Java and disembarked in the city of Semarang. There he enrolled in an academy for foreign languages and chose English as his major.

James lived in a dorm exclusively for Papuan

James Wambrauw as a young man

university students studying in Semarang. Many differences exist between Papuans from the eastern edge of Indonesia and the Javanese from the west. The Javanese are slight of body and extremely polite, reserved and soft-spoken. The Papuans tend to be larger, louder, and more loquacious. And they are well known as skilled fighters. James himself was a brown belt in karate. Living in the dorm with other native Papuans, James naturally spent a lot of time with them. Soon they became infamous in Semarang as drinkers and fighters who wise people tried to avoid.

Another difference between the Papuans and the Javanese is religion. Java is predominantly Muslim, and Papua is predominantly Christian. James grew up as a nominal Christian. He was an excellent musician and loved to play his guitar and sing. When James arrived in Semarang, he frequently attended

14

church and often sang and played his guitar. But on weekdays he began to provide music in the local bars and nightclubs. Soon James was so busy singing in nightclubs that he dropped out of school.

By this time James had enough English proficiency to obtain a job as a switchboard operator in a large hotel. One day, an American pastor and his wife were passing through Semarang and checked into the hotel where James worked. They stayed for several days and got to know James personally. They were impressed with him. The evening before their departure, they felt compelled to talk with James about his soul. Late that night, after James was done working, this pastor and his wife witnessed to James and led him to a personal saving knowledge of Christ.

The next day the American pastor and his wife checked out of the hotel and continued on their journey. But they left a letter for James that went something like this:

James,

We are so happy that you have accepted Christ as your personal Savior. We know you have a bright future ahead of you in the hotel business or any other business you might choose. But James, we are concerned. While you sit here in this air-conditioned hotel, hundreds and thousands of your fellow countrymen are lost and dying and slipping off into an eternity without Christ. They desperately need someone to tell them about Jesus. We think maybe God is calling you to be that person.

James didn't know what to make of the letter. But the more he thought about it, the more it seemed like this was what God was calling him to do. He knew that if he was going to become a preacher he would need to go to a Bible college. So he asked around and found the address of a well-known Bible college in East Java. He sent off an application but was very disappointed when they didn't accept him. Then he learned of another Bible college just outside of Semarang and thought this was why God had closed the first door. So he applied at this school, but again the reply was the same—they would not accept James as a student to prepare for the ministry. James was in great turmoil. He felt God was calling him, and he knew he must prepare, but every time he tried to enroll in a Bible school the door closed. Maybe it wasn't God's will after all. He just didn't know what to do.

Things finally came to a head one day, and James felt like this was "D Day"—Decision Day. He asked off work, returned to his dorm, and told his friends he had an important decision to make that afternoon. He didn't want to be disturbed. In his room, James closed the door and began to wrestle over God's will for his life. He hadn't been there long when there was a knock on the door. James ignored it because of his previous instructions. But the knock came again. Finally James brusquely called out, "Who is it and what do you want?"

"It's Henry," came the reply. "We used to sing together in churches here in Semarang several years ago."

James had to think before he remembered Henry. He hadn't seen him in several years. Finally James invited him in, and they began to visit. After a while James asked why Henry had come. Henry was a little uncomfortable, but began. "This morning when I woke up, I felt impressed to come talk with you today. So I got on a bus and rode three hours to come here. I have only one question to ask you. Would you consider joining me as a student at my school?"

"Where are you studying?" James wanted to know.

"I'm a student at the Indonesia Nazarene Theological College (INTC) in Yogyakarta, and I am preparing for the ministry."

James was stunned. He realized this had to be more than mere coincidence. On the very day he was going to make his final decision about his future Henry just "happened" to show up. So James began to ply him with questions about INTC and about the Church of the Nazarene. He liked everything he heard.

James accompanied Henry back to the school to be interviewed. After sharing his testimony, he was accepted as a student. INTC uses a two-pronged approach to teaching: principles and practical application. Monday through Friday instructors give lectures, tests, and assignments. On Saturday and Sunday, the students fan out into the surrounding areas and put to practical use what they have been taught in class.

When it came time for James to take a ministry assignment, he was sent to pioneer a church in a city about an hour's bus ride away. He began by meeting the people. Soon he started a Sunday School, then added a home Bible study class, and suddenly a new church plant was born. It was exciting to hear his stories of the miracles of God's grace. Perhaps the story that best represents his work there actually happened on his way back to the school. When he arrived in Yogyakarta, it was so late that the city buses had quit running. So he bargained for a *becak* (bicycle pedicab) to take him to the campus. When he climbed into the *becak,* the driver began to work James for a good tip. James promised to give him something "extra" when they got to the campus. When they arrived, James went into the kitchen, poured a cool glass of water, and brought it to the tired, sweaty, and thirsty *becak* driver. While the man was gulping down the water, James said, "Say, I know of water that will cause a man never to thirst again."

"Oh? What kind of water is that?" the driver queried.

"Come over here and I will tell you," James replied.

There on the front porch of the school building, late on a Sunday night, James shared the gospel with this *becak* driver. That night he not only drank cool, clean water from the kitchen, he also drank deeply from the well of eternal water.

After James graduated from INTC, he went to Asia-Pacific Nazarene Theological Seminary (APNTS) in Manila, Philippines. He excelled in all areas there—campus leadership, academics, and ministry. Upon graduation, he returned to Indonesia and began to teach at his alma mater, sharing his burden of reaching his country for Christ with the next generation of young Indonesians. He quickly rose in competence, influence, and position—teacher, then dean of students, and finally president of INTC.

But all along James told us his real heart's desire was to return to his home island of Biak to tell his family about Christ. We committed with him that when God opened the door we would do our

All along James told us his real heart's desire was to return to his home island of Biak to tell his family about Christ.

best to support him. In the meantime we needed him to help us at INTC.

A few years ago God did open that door. So far, all of the Nazarene work has been coordinated out of the city of Yogyakarta, but for some time we sensed the need to open up a second hub in the eastern part of Indonesia. The logical place was Jayapura, in James's home province of Papua. We had already established an INTC extension education center there with a good response from the people. After much prayer and thought, we approached James with the proposal that he resign as president of INTC and return to his home province to lead the Nazarene work. He asked for a week to pray about it but came back the next day saying he was ready to go.

In August of 2002, James, Enny, and their three children packed up and moved to James's home province. James is presently serving as the district superintendent of our newly formed Papua District. He is also serving as head of our extension school and planting a new church in a suburb of Jayapura. Several times he has been able to return to his home island of Biak and preach the gospel to his family.

Two generations ago Insan Brasi, machete in hand, walked the dusty trails of Biak looking for heads. Now his grandson, James Wambrauw, walks those same dusty trails, God's Word in hand, hunting hearts.

James and Enny Wambrauw

Missions Update

The Church of the Nazarene has always carried a missionary vision for the far regions of Indonesia. We began work on the main island of Java in 1973. In the 1980s we spread out to the surrounding islands of Bali, Sumatra, Kalimantan (Borneo), and Papua (Irian Jaya). In 1999 we organized Kalimantan and Papua, and sent our first Indonesian missionary, Acy Lodja, to the newly independent country of East Timor in 2002. Pray with us now about how to best reach Malaysia, Singapore, and Brunei.

"Therefore go and make disciples of all nations"
(Matt. 28:19*a*).

Pepi Causing
PHILIPPINES

Tillie and I were living in the port city of Iloilo when I received a letter from John Pattee, a fellow missionary living at Luzon Nazarene Bible College (LNBC) on the main island of the Philippines. He asked if I had a target location for a church plant in my area. If so, he wanted to come during the semester break and hold a joint evangelistic campaign with me there. I replied that I did have such a place and invited him to come to the small rural village of Mongorocoro.

John arrived by ship, and I picked him up in my car to take him to Mongorocoro. The road leading to the village was not exactly a super highway. We dodged rocks larger than the car, holes deeper than my height, and ruts that were inescapable if a wheel slipped in. Eventually we reached Mongorocoro in one piece. We then presented ourselves to the barrio lieutenant to receive permission to minister in his city. He helped us locate a home that would serve as both our living quarters and a sanctuary. In the front yard we set up a long bamboo pole for the altar. We didn't need to find benches for the people because we knew it was customary for them to bring their own benches, chairs, upended boxes, and five-gallon oil cans to sit on. We hung a flip chart for the song book and lit a lantern for light while John played the accordion for music. Then using film strips of different Bible stories together with good holiness preaching, we launched the evangelistic campaign.

Early in the first week a young man came. He stood close to the front of the crowd, and in his shirt pocket I noticed what looked like a small New Testament. I nudged John in the side and told him a Christian young man was present. After the service I quickly went to meet him. I learned his name was Pepi. "Are you a Christian?" I asked.

He looked at me and said, "No, sir. Why do you ask?"

I told him I had seen the New Testament in his shirt pocket and thought perhaps he was already a believer. Young Pepi said that when he was a small boy, the Gideons had come to his school in Mongorocoro and given each of the students a New Testament. He had kept it since then and brought it with him to the service. I thank God for the Gideons who give Bibles to our children in the Philippines.

Pepi came back every night, always with that little New Testament in his pocket. Then came the night when he knelt at that bamboo altar and accepted Jesus as his Lord and Savior. Three weeks sped by so quickly it seemed, and the evangelistic campaign was soon over. John and I returned to our homes and to our separate duties.

Not much later I received a letter from the Bible college asking if I had any prospective students for their upcoming semester. I remembered Pepi Causing back at Mongorocoro. I drove back down that arduous road and found Pepi tending the vegetables on his parents' small farm.

"Pepi, would you like to go to the Nazarene Bible College on Luzon?" I inquired. "You could learn more about the Bible and study English as well."

Pepi said he would like that very much, but his parents would have to approve. Immediately we went to see them and asked if it might be agreeable with them for their son to enroll in our Bible school. They gave their permission, and Pepi soon packed up and left for LNBC.

Early in the semester a great revival swept through the campus, and Pepi became established in the Lord and felt called to preach. Those were good days for him. He was receiving a quality education and being nurtured by godly teachers. As his freshman year came to a close, Pepi began to look forward to the summer break and what he would do during that time. His heart was burning for God. He knew he must preach, and most importantly, he wanted to reach his family and his own people for Christ. They had no church, no place to meet to learn about God. So he approached the school authorities with the request to be allowed to return home for the summer months between school years. Unfortunately, many good, God-called young men and women went back to their barrio culture before they were truly grounded in their faith. They succumbed to peer pressure at home and never made it back to the Bible school. So the administrators told him they didn't feel this was a good idea.

But Pepi's heart continued to burn with this deep desire. Every day he went to the school authorities and pleaded, "Please, let me return home for the summer months to preach to my people." But the answer continued to be no. This went on for quite a while until one day someone in authority finally said, "Let's think about it." That was enough for Pepi. He went to his dorm room, packed his belongings, and came back ready to go. He promised to return and to be faithful to the Lord and His call to prepare for the ministry. With that he was allowed to go. The school gave him a small amount of Alabaster money to erect a temporary structure to serve as a gathering place for his people, and Pepi went home.

Pepi Causing with missionary Bob McCroskey Sr.

With the Alabaster money and the help of his family and friends, Pepi built a small grass and bamboo church and began to tell his people about the love of God. Preaching just on Sundays to those who came to church was not enough; he felt he had to do more. So Pepi began going up and down the road looking for children, young people, and adults to whom he could tell the story of Jesus. His passion for Christ burned deep within him. One day he found a small farming village just off the main road that seemed an ideal place to begin a church plant. There were many people of all ages there. He located the barrio leaders and asked if he could begin coming on Sunday afternoons to hold a children's Sunday School class. They gave their permission. After preaching in his Sunday morning service in Mongorocoro, Pepi then boarded public transportation to the small village of Mansun-sun and began his outreach Sunday School class.

One Sunday afternoon, as Pepi was closing the lesson, he noticed several adults standing around, listening. Instead of dismissing the children with prayer, Pepi began to preach to the adults. He opened his Bible to the story of the prodigal son and contextualized it to their setting. He spoke of a young man from the barrio who came to his father asking if he could have his inheritance and go to Manila (the capital city of the Philippines). He was tired of planting rice. He wanted something more exciting—a taste of city life. The sad-hearted father reluctantly gave him his share of the inheritance, and with great anticipation the young man boarded a ship to Manila to enjoy his good fortune.

Before long, however, the young man was out of money and out of friends. Things went from bad to worse until he finally took a job feeding pigs to stay alive. There the memories of home flooded his mind. How he missed his father! He was tired of his low life in the city. He made up his mind to return home, and soon he was back in the protective arms of his father. Then Pepi added, "I wonder if some-one here has become tired of life as it is and would like to come home to the Father."

In one of the thatch huts clustered about the open area where Pepi was preaching, an old woman lay on her grass mat. She hoisted her frail body on her elbow, thrust her hand through the open window, and called out, "I would, Pastor. I would!"

The priest said the problem was an evil spirit in my house, and it would only leave if I burned my house down.

Young Pepi quickly dismissed the people and hurried around the little house and up the ladder to where the old woman lay.

"Come in, Pastor," she said, "and forgive my old house. I used to a have a good home," she continued, "but when I could no longer walk my sons took me to many doctors and healers for a cure. When they couldn't help me, my sons took me to a priest. He said the problem was an evil spirit in my house, and it would only leave if I burned my house down. Pastor, my sons brought me home, and we talked together as a family. We decided it would be good if I could walk again, so one of my sons carried me out of my good house, laid me on a grassy spot, and took a torch to my home. As we watched my house burn, we all thought that soon I would be able to walk again. But, Pastor, when the ashes turned cold, I still could not walk. Not only was my home destroyed, but my hope was as well."

Young Pepi told the woman more about Jesus and His love. She then accepted Him as her Lord

A house on stilts in the Philippines

and Savior, and her life was changed. She began to hunger and thirst after righteousness and asked Pepi to return often and tell her more from the Bible. So every week Pepi made the trip just to feed the hungry heart of this little old woman.

One day, in a simple Bible study, Pepi began to tell this woman and the people she had brought into her home about faith—that God would do great things for them if they would have faith in Him. Then he closed his Bible, put it into his brief-case, and prepared to leave. But the little old woman was not finished. "Wait, Pastor, tell me more about this faith," she said. This was all that young pastor needed as he began to expound on the concept of faith and what it could do in our lives. He said if they had the faith of even just a small grain of mustard seed, then God would do great things for them and through them.

The old woman asked, "If I had faith, could I walk again?" Pepi laid his hands on her and prayed the prayer of faith.

Pepi soon called me to come to Monsunsun for a revival. I happily agreed and boarded a beat-up, old, rickety bus. Pepi met me at the crossing to help me carry my things. A little ways down the dirt road I saw the cloud of dust and knew the children were on their way to greet us. As we got closer, and the dust settled a bit, I could see a little old woman making her way toward us. As she came closer I asked, "Pepi, who is that?"

"Oh, Brother McCroskey, that is the old woman I have been telling you about, the one who could not walk. Ever since the day I laid hands on her and prayed the prayer of faith she has been walking more and more. Every day she comes out to meet me."

As she neared us, I could see she was carrying a small bag of rice and a chicken. She gave the rice to the pastor and the chicken to me and said, "Thank you for coming to tell my people about Jesus."

That night under the stars we prepared for the service—the bamboo pole, the lantern, and the flip chart. We were ready. Pepi played his accordion, and the revival was on its way. We sang, I preached a simple gospel message, and Pepi translated my words into the local dialect. At the close of the service, we sang a chorus of invitation. As we did, the little old woman began to go back and forth among that great crowd. She brought 19 people to kneel at our bamboo pole altar. They were all her grandchildren.

Yes, missions is people. It is training young men and women to become preachers and pastors who take the light of the gospel to thousands of their countrymen who need to know Jesus.

Missions Update

The Church of the Nazarene has always emphasized the planting of churches in new areas. Several key targets we are focusing on now include the islands of Palawan, Leyte, Samar, Negros, Panay, and Mindanao, as well as the providences of Pagasinan, Quezon, and Metro Manila on the main island of Luzon. Our goal is to have a Nazarene church in each of the 34,000 barangays (communities) scattered throughout the 7,100 islands of the Philippines.

Filipino Nazarenes also have a vision for the lost in other countries. In 1977, three medical missionaries went to Swaziland from the Philippines: Drs. Ben and Mary Nacionales and Dr. Norma Bajoyo. A nurse, Lily Sinot, went to Papua New Guinea. Presently, Rex Ray and Pearl de la Peret serve as missionaries to Micronesia.

3

"Whatever you do, do it all for the glory of God" (1 Cor. 10:31*b*).

Yez
INDONESIA

Just a dime and a prayer. That's all it took to trigger a remarkable chain of events still growing in the life of Yez.

Yez was born in Ambarawa, Central Java, in 1973. His family was Muslim, typical in this country as Indonesia is the largest Muslim nation in the world. When Yez reached high school, a rift developed between him and his parents. They felt they had a teenage son who was out of control, and Yez felt he had parents who didn't understand him or care much about him. So Yez left home and took to the streets just like several of his friends.

In Indonesia, street people are common. They are often young people and children who have left home for various reasons to make a living on the street. Some scavenge paper, bottles, and cans from the garbage to sell to recyclers. Some turn to crime, robbing people or homes. Many, though, become street musicians who sing for money. A ukulele, or maybe a guitar, serves as accompaniment. Most street musicians play much simpler instruments, one of the most common being a *kicik-kicik*. This is a small block of wood on which are loosely nailed three or four sets of flattened pop bottle lids. When the wood is shaken, the lids rattle against each other becoming a percussion instrument.

Instruments in hand, these street musicians ply their trade. Sometimes they go from house to house or business to business singing until someone within earshot can tolerate no more and pays them to leave. Or they wait at stoplights, serenading occupants in the cars. The Ambarawa method was to work the buses passing through the city.

Yez soon mastered the tricks of the trade. Every day he would take his guitar, board a bus, and work his way down the aisle, playing his guitar and singing for money. Most peo-

Yez

33

ple gave him a small coin, the equivalent of a penny or less. One day, however, a passenger gave him a 1,000 rupiah bill, the equivalent of a dime, and invited him to visit his house sometime. Yez about dropped his guitar he was so startled at the large amount. He wondered if perhaps there might be more money where this came from and didn't wait long before he visited this generous man. His curiosity doubled when the address turned out to be a church, and the benefactor a pastor.

Yez was not at all interested in Christianity for he had been taught that it was the white man's religion. However, Rev. Sukarli, the pastor, was so kind to him that Yez kept coming back. Rev. Sukarli began to teach Yez how to play an electric guitar. In the course of his guitar training sessions, Rev. Sukarli witnessed to Yez. Three months later, Yez accepted Christ as his personal Savior.

When Yez graduated from high school, Rev. Sukarli helped him obtain a job in a Christian printing company. One day he picked up a book they were printing and read the following verse: "The harvest is plentiful, but the workers are few" (Luke 10:2a). Intrigued, he took the book home to read and soon felt God calling him into the ministry.

When Yez first accepted Christ, his parents didn't mind much. But when he said he was going to enroll in a Bible school to prepare for the ministry, they became angry. They knew pastors make little money and were counting on Yez to provide for them in their old age. But Yez felt sure God had called him, so he made plans to enroll in a Bible school. He had an uncle who had just graduated from the Indonesia Nazarene Theological College and strongly encouraged Yez to enroll there. He did, but it was not easy for him. His parents continued to oppose his choice and were not willing to send him money for school expenses. Thankfully, God brought other encouragers into his life—his uncle, his grandparents who were Christians, and Rev. Sukarli.

Yez worked hard in school, and he always came to class with a big smile. But academic studies were not his strength. When taking exams, he struggled painfully to answer the questions. He was constantly on the borderline between passing and failing. Sometimes he wondered if he would even make it in the ministry.

When it came time for Yez to begin his practical ministry, the district gave him a weekend assignment in a city on the northern coast of Java. The district was close to shutting down that church for a variety of reasons. First, the church had experienced a series of poor pastors, and attendance had decreased to the point that there were only two faithful families left. Second, that part of Java, the north central coast, is notorious for its resistance to the

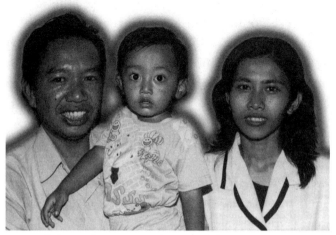
Yez with his wife, Arni, and son, Yoel

gospel. In fact, shortly before Yez was assigned there, the local village leaders had declared our church off-limits for religious activities because neighbors had protested services being held in their community. Finally, it was a five-hour bus trip for Yez to get there from the Bible school.

But Yez believed God could build a church in that city. He felt this was God's harvest field for him and that God had a special plan for this church.

The first challenge Yez faced was locating a place to worship. The only place available was a chicken coop—literally. So that's where they began. During Sunday services, the chickens were shooed to the side, and the congregation sat in the middle.

If they could've counted chickens instead of people for Sunday morning attendance, they would have had some impressive numbers!

Thus, Yez began his ministry. It was a time of struggle. During the week, he worked hard on his studies. Then each Friday he got on the bus and endured the long ride. The struggle continued at his small church. The people were few. The offerings were minimal. Yez himself had almost no money. The church had little furniture, so he slept on the floor using his Sunday clothes as his pillow. On Sundays, he simply unrolled his pillow, put on the clothes, and led the service.

But God blessed them abundantly. He gave that church powerful and unique ways to reach out to their community. And the church began to grow.

One of the most effective evangelism tools they used was the *JESUS* film. Most of the film showings in Indonesia have been in private homes using a DVD player and TV. But Yez and his team made a contact in a nearby village and obtained permission to show the film in front of the town hall using a 16-mm projector. They were elated. On the day of the showing, however, they learned this building didn't have enough electricity to run the projector. Yez was terribly disappointed. Then one of the leading Muslim men of the community, *a kyai,* stepped in to offer his home and yard as an alternate venue for the showing. His name was Mr. K and his business, coincidentally, was renting sound systems for social events in the community. He offered the team free use of his sound system and told them he could provide adequate electrical power for the projector. What an offer! As Kyai K watched the film that night, he just stood there crying, wondering how it could be that an innocent man was crucified. Yez began to make regular visits to this village to disciple some of the people who had made decisions for Christ. Not long afterward, Kyai K notified Yez that he, too, wanted to follow Jesus. So Yez led him to the Lord. While the church rejoiced in this conversion, the surrounding Muslim community became irritated. They met at the town hall with the intention of "correcting" this situation. Kyai K was called in and asked if he had been forced to become a Christian. He said no. They called in Yez and asked him if he had somehow tricked or lured Kyai K into becoming a Christian. But Yez told them all he had done was tell Kyai K about Jesus. In the end, the community decided they would have to accept this. But they didn't like it and often subjected Kyai K to intimidation and persecution so he would recant his faith. Kyai K has stood firm. We now have a Nazarene church planted in that village pastored by a layman from Yez's home church.

Perhaps Yez's most outstanding evangelistic gift

is how he ministers to those the world tends to just pass by unnoticed. One Saturday night he couldn't sleep and felt impressed by the Lord to go down to the city train station. When he arrived late that night, he saw many street people, even families, who were literally living in the train station. Some were sleeping in the station, some in idle boxcars, and some on the ground underneath stationary boxcars. Yez remembered his own early days as a street musician when he was living on the street like this, and his heart strings began to hum. He recognized an opportunity for ministry among people who had been sidelined by life.

Perhaps Yez's most outstanding evangelistic gift is how he ministers to those the world tends to just pass by unnoticed.

Yez also realized that if he was going to have a ministry to these street people, he would have to become one of them. So one day he dressed in his oldest clothes, walked down to the train station, guitar in hand, and began to befriend them. In his days as a street musician, he had plied the buses, but here the musicians worked the trains passing through town. They would board the train then work their way down the aisles singing and playing for money. When the train reached the next city, they got off, pooled the money they had collected, bought food and ate a communal meal in the station. When the next train came through going the opposite direction, they got on and sang their way back home. The money they raised was just enough to buy simple, daily meals. Yez shared his money and their food together with them.

When he felt the time was right, Yez began to witness to the street people. Since he had already won their friendship and trust by living together with them, they listened to what he had to say. They didn't know he was a pastor of a local church or that he involved his church in providing meals to street kids and other castaways in the community. Yez formed a cell group among these street people and one by one began to lead them to the Lord Jesus Christ.

Sadly, a few years ago, a terrible train wreck occurred on the northern route. Nearly 100 people were killed. Yez had ridden that very train himself, singing and asking for money with his street friends. The accident happened in the late afternoon, and Yez knew in his heart that some of his street friends had been involved in the crash. They would have been on their way back home after a day of singing on the trains. When Yez went to the morgue, he identified the bodies of 15 kids he had been discipling. Because the accident had been so horrific, he couldn't recognize them from their faces. He recognized them from their clothes. Most of them had only one set of clothes they wore day after day. In fact, several of them were wearing clothes Yez had given them. No one came to claim the bodies. No one cared enough about them to even check on them. Their own families had completely lost track of them.

In Indonesia, funeral homes are rare. When someone dies, the family buys a simple casket and prepares the body for burial themselves. After two days of fruitlessly waiting for families to come and claim the bodies, Yez and his church members took on the job. They couldn't afford caskets, so they bought material to wrap the bodies. They transported them to the grave site and took turns carrying the bodies from the car. They buried them, sometimes with multiple bodies in the same grave. It was a sad day. So many of Yez's friends were gone at such a young age. But what a joy it was for Yez to remember the occasions when he had led most of these boys to the Lord. They are in a far better world now than they had ever lived in during this life.

Jim Elliot, who was martyred by the Indians in Peru, wrote in his daybook, "Lord, I don't want to be just a signpost on the road pointing people to Christ. Instead I want to be a fork in the road bringing them to a commitment." I think this describes Pastor Yez's ministry quite well.

Missions Update

Yez is one of many pastors who use the JESUS film with good results. Due to the restrictions in Indonesia, we developed a unique strategy that involves local teams tied to individual churches. At the time of this writing, 39 teams have shown the JESUS film 3,879 times with 30,156 viewers, 10,853 decisions for Christ, and 8,440 people requesting discipleship follow-up.

"Whatever you do, do it all for the glory of God"
(1 Cor. 10:31*b*).

Eva
PHILIPPINES

A few years ago, a small church in Oklahoma asked Tillie and me to speak at a Faith Promise convention. We enjoy going to these services as they provide a little more time for us to be with the people of the church. I make it a habit to ask the pastor what the church's goal is and how they are planning to allocate the money that will be raised. When we arrived at this particular church, I quickly saw I didn't need to ask these questions. Stretched across the front of the platform was a banner with the words "FAITH PROMISE" written on it. Underneath this they had listed the ways in which they would allocate that year's offerings. The first item listed was the General Budget (now known as the World Evangelism Fund). Without this fund we never could have been missionaries, had national pastors, or built churches. It is the lifeline for Nazarene missionary work.

The list included other significant items as well, including medical and Alabaster offerings. But it was the last item on the list that caught my attention: Radio Offering—$5. My impression was not that the church didn't believe in the radio offering, but rather it simply wasn't a top priority for them. After all, everyone has a television, don't they? Actually, in our part of the world, the important thing is that little black box we call the transistor radio.

Some of the larger cities in the Philippines have the luxury of newspapers. But in the surrounding village areas, the radio is the chief means of mass communication. You can hear the radios as the farmers carry them to the fields while they plant rice. You can hear them as the women take them to the markets to buy and sell. You can pick up various radio stations as you walk the crowded streets of the cities. It seems as if radios in the city have two positions on the volume control: off and loud. Five houses down from us, our neighbor enjoyed listening to his radio, and everyone nearby had full advantage of the broadcast too. The radio's availability and wide range makes it a great tool for evangelism on the 7,100 islands that make up the Philippines.

Since many of our pastors are located in distant and isolated places, they treasure any opportunity to congregate with fellow Nazarenes. One of the most significant opportunities for fellowship is the pastors and wives retreat. For one of these retreats, we invited a nationally known radio preacher named

Hahn Browne to be our special speaker. Hahn works with DZAS, a Christian radio station located north of Manila. What a blessing he was at the retreat. On the following Monday morning, Rev. Browne needed a ride back to Manila. One of our Nazarene missionaries offered to drive him. It would be an all-day trip.

About halfway to Manila, the duo arrived in the town of Moncada. They were tired and thirsty, so they decided to stop to stretch and get something to drink. They parked the car under a big acacia tree in front of a small bamboo house, then bought a couple of warm cokes from a nearby outdoor stall. As the two men stood in the shade of the tree enjoying their drinks, they noticed a teenage girl looking at them from the window of a nearby house. The missionary observed a book on the window ledge and asked, "Young lady, tell me, would that black book happen to be a Bible?"

The girl replied, "Oh, sir, there is no evangelical church here in Moncada. If I want to go to church, I just turn on my radio."

She picked it up and said, "Indeed it is, sir. That's my Bible."

"Are you a Christian?" the missionary asked.

"Yes, sir, I am a Christian."

"Where do you go to church?"

"Oh, sir, there is no evangelical church here in Moncada. If I want to go to church, I just turn on my radio."

Mr. Browne then asked, "Would you happen to know the name of Hahn Browne?"

"Yes," she said, "he is a speaker on DZAS. I listen to him all the time."

He then told her that he was Hahn Browne. Now her curiosity was really piqued, so she came down the ladder of her tiny bamboo house to visit with the two gentlemen. (In the Philippines, many houses are built on stilts either to guard against floods or to provide storage and additional space for the family members.) She told them her name was Eva. The missionary asked Eva if she was certain there was no evangelical church in Moncada. Once more she assured them there was none. She added that when she wanted to learn a new gospel song, she would just turn on her radio and sing along with it. Then she added with great emotion, "I got saved listening to my radio!"

The missionary told her there was a Nazarene church about 30 minutes down the road and that he would ask the pastor in that town to come to Moncada and hold a Bible study. "Would you like that?" he asked. Eva assured him not only would she be happy for the pastor to come, but she would bring friends and neighbors for him to teach as well. A plan was set in motion. The men said good-bye to their new friend and continued on to the nearby town of Paniqui.

They stopped at the parsonage of the Nazarene church and called out a greeting to the pastor. Pastor Rudy emerged and came down the bamboo ladder of the home. The two visitors greeted the pastor and told him about the young girl in Moncada. They asked if he would travel there to conduct a Bible study for her and her friends. The pastor said he would love to. Thus began Pastor Rudy's weekly 25-mile treks to Moncada on his bicycle to unfold the Word of God with Eva and her family and friends.

On my following furlough, a family in Nebraska gave me a small motor that sits on the wheel of a bicycle. I took it to Pastor Rudy, and he attached it to his bicycle to create a makeshift moped. As Pastor Rudy sped down the road every week, God blessed the small harvest in Moncada.

Some weeks later, I was holding a revival in Paniqui. While I was there, I asked the pastor about the progress of the work in Moncada and if any Christians from that town would be attending the revival. He assured me they had already made arrangements to hire a passenger jeep to bring them to the Sunday morning service. All week long we had a wonderful revival meeting and looked forward to the closing service on Sunday. When it finally

A passenger jeep in the Philippines

came, the pastor and I sat on the platform waiting for the people to come in from their Sunday School classes. These were generally held under a large mango tree or in the shade of the church building. Soon we saw a jeep stop in front of the church. The pastor leaned over to me to say that the people from Moncada had arrived. Sure enough, Eva got out of the jeep along with 18 other adults, young people, and children. Then Eva stepped up into the jeep and helped an old man with thick glasses and a cane totter out of the jeep. The pastor leaned over to me and said, "Brother McCroskey, that's Eva's grandfather. He is more than 80 years old, and this is the first time he has set foot in a Protestant church."

Eva walked with her grandfather up the single

aisle of the church, led him to a bench second from the front, then sat across the aisle from him (it is customary for men and women to sit on opposite sides of the church in the Philippines).

I preached a simple gospel message and gave an invitation. The congregation stood and sang "Just As I Am" so beautifully. Before my eyes a precious sight unfolded. Eva stepped across the aisle of that little church, placed her arm around the shoulders of her grandfather, and asked if he would like to become a Christian. The old man bowed his head and nodded. Eva slipped her arm into his, and slowly the two of them made their way to the altar. Then Eva stood beside her grandfather as he coaxed his old knees to bow to a living Savior—knees that had previously bowed to an idol in his home for many years. It was my privilege to kneel on the other side of him and tell him more fully the story of Jesus. Eva's grandfather has since gone to be with the Lord, but I couldn't help but think what a marvelous investment that five-dollar radio offering was from that small church in Oklahoma.

The Lord blessed the work in Moncada, and soon they needed a full-time pastor. A church in the United States gave a small sum of money that was used to build a cement block church in Moncada. The pastor, Rev. Bustamante, invited me to come for a revival. While I was there, he told me about a vil-

The Tolega church congregation

lage named Tolega in the country where members of the community had asked him to help build a small church. Working together, they had gathered bamboo poles and palm leaves and created a simple structure that included bamboo seats and an altar. They soon asked me to come and hold an evangelistic campaign there also. On the closing Sunday, I organized the church with 21 charter members. Today we have two fully functioning churches in that area—one in the town of Moncada and another in the village of Tolega. This all happened because a teenage girl had a transistor radio, listened to it, and was saved.

The Church of the Nazarene is investing more money in radio evangelism now than ever before. Radio waves easily pass through barriers of bamboo, rock, and steel to reach hearts in the most inaccessible corners of the world. I truly believe the radio offering is more vital and a more worthy investment today than ever before in the history of our denomination.

Missions Update

Radio has been a key evangelistic tool for the Church of the Nazarene in the Philippine Islands. Currently we are producing 7 radio programs in 3 languages and broadcasting these programs in 15 geographic areas and major cities. In one quarter alone, more than 2,380 people responded to these Nazarene broadcasts.

> "But just as you excel in everything . . . see that you also excel in this grace of giving" (2 Cor. 8:7).

Pak Karjan
INDONESIA

During one of our furloughs, I [Bob Jr.] was speaking on the East Coast when a tall, rawboned, sandy-haired young man approached me at the end of the service. We shook hands, and I noted his grip was hard, his hand thickly calloused. He then reached into his back pocket, pulled out his wallet, and opened it. It held a single $10 bill. The man handed the money to me and said, "This is for Indonesia." I looked at him, noticing his clothes were clean and neatly pressed but not the best. His grip was hard and rough, and I knew he worked hard. I took a step back and said, "No, I don't want to take your money. I know you need it. God will provide in other ways." But with tears in his eyes, he insisted, "God talked to my heart this evening, and I have to give you this money." As I pocketed that $10, I prayed that God would help me wisely and profitably invest what I knew had been so sacrificially given.

Not long after that, Rosa and I returned to Indonesia. As I thought and prayed about how I would use the money, I decided I would invest it in the ministry of Pak (Mr.) Karjan.

When God called Pak Karjan, he was working as a *kernet,* or general helper, on a truck crew. His most important job was to start the truck. Before you begin to think too lightly of his skills, this truck was manufactured prior to the days of push-button or turnkey starters. Instead, it had to be started with a crank. One day, when Pak Karjan tried to start the truck, he lost his grip on the crank. It spun back, hit him on the mouth, and knocked out his top four front teeth. It also knocked him out. The other crew members dragged him over to the side of the road to recuperate and called on *kernet* No. 2 to start the truck. He, too, lost his grip on the crank, causing it to spin back and hit him on his head. But instead of just losing teeth, he lost his life.

Pak Karjan blurted out, "I nearly died today, and I know I am not ready to meet God. Can you tell me how I can be ready?"

That night when Pak Karjan returned home, everyone wanted to hear how he lost his teeth. Among them was a neighbor who was a Christian pastor. After listening to the story, the pastor just shook his head and said, "Wow, you were really lucky, Pak Karjan. You just lost your teeth; your friend lost his life. That could have happened to you." Then he looked Pak Karjan in the eye and asked, "If it had been you, where would you be right now? Are you ready to meet God?" Pak Karjan was a Muslim. The Muslim faith is basically a works religion—followers hope their good works outweigh their bad works in the end. Assurance of salvation is nonexistent for them. That night as Pak Karjan tried to sleep, he tossed and turned as his mind replayed the day's events. His brush with death had been so close. And most frightening of all was that he knew he wasn't ready to meet God. Finally, he could take it no longer. He got up, went over to his neighbor's home, and knocked on the door. When his friend opened the door, Pak Karjan blurted out, "I nearly died today, and I know I am not ready to meet God. Can you tell me how I can be ready?"

That night, with the guidance of his neighbor, Pak Karjan accepted Jesus Christ as his personal Savior. Soon after that he began a time of intense Bible study. Every night after work, Pak Karjan would go to the pastor's home where they would spend several hours, side-by-side, studying God's Word. About three months later, Pak Karjan told the pastor he felt God was calling him into the ministry. He wondered if the pastor could help him find a place to serve. Soon the pastor's church offered Pak Karjan a post up in the mountain village of Gendurit, located in a remote and dangerous area. With no public transportation available, Pak Karjan had to walk 11 miles each way. But he never complained. Instead, he was thrilled with the chance to share the gospel with those who had never heard it.

God began to bless Pak Karjan's ministry in this village. The little community of believers began to grow until soon 40 people were meeting regularly. The Muslim majority in the community was not happy to see a church growing in their midst, so they began to look for a way to stop it. And the opportunity came. At that time Indonesia was holding national elections, and one of the laws stated there could be no political gatherings without a police permit. So the village elders reported that Pak Karjan was holding a political meeting without a permit. The police swooped in and took him to jail. The small group of believers in Gendurit prayed fervently for God to deliver their pastor. They sent word down to the mother church in the lowlands, and the Christian family there also gathered in prayer. Meanwhile, Pak Karjan sat in jail until finally the captain called him in to ask why he was in Gendurit. That was all the prompting Pak Karjan needed to begin witnessing to the police captain. When the man was finally able to get a word in edgewise, he told Pak Karjan no crime had been committed and he was free to go. Furthermore, he added, he should continue to preach the gospel because the people needed to hear it.

During this time, Mrs. Karjan was still a Muslim and opposed to what her husband was doing. But God was also working in her life. One day she became sick and soon fell seriously ill. Thinking she was dying, the family was called home. Pak Karjan went to his pastor friend's home and asked him to come over and pray that God would heal his wife. The pastor came, prayed, and God answered. Mrs. Karjan knew God had done a miracle in her life. Not long after that she invited Jesus into her heart. She began to do everything she could to encourage and assist her husband; she was the perfect help-mate for him. They complemented each other's weaknesses with their own strengths and seemed to be a perfectly matched pair. This was evident all the way down to the fact that Pak Karjan was missing his top four front teeth, and his wife was missing her bottom four front teeth!

A couple months later, Pak Karjan told his pastor friend he felt God leading him in a new direction. "God has blessed us in Gendurit," he said. "When I first went there, there was no one, but now we have a strong church. They need someone better trained to pastor them. I have no education." And then with a twinkle in his eye he added, "Besides,

God has called me to be a pioneer. I want to go somewhere where there is no church and start one."

Pak Karjan felt led of God to move to the city of Magelang. There he found work in a chrome shop and began looking and praying for a church-planting opportunity. He began setting aside small

Pak Karjan

amounts of money to use whenever God opened the door. But he also looked around for open doors nearby. He befriended a young coworker named Siswiyono and led him to the Lord one day after work. There followed in this young man's life the same hunger and thirst to know more about his newfound faith that Pak Karjan had felt after his own conversion. So every evening after work, the two men sat side-by-side to study God's Word. Except now Pak Karjan was no longer the student; he was the teacher sharing with Siswiyono the truths he had learned.

One evening, Siswiyono came to Pak Karjan with a faraway look in his eyes. He began to talk about his family who lived in a village a three-hour bus ride away. "I know this is asking a lot," he began, "but I wonder if you would be willing to go home with me some weekend and tell my folks about Jesus. No one has ever come to our village to share the gospel."

When Pak Karjan heard that invitation, his eyes lit up and he agreed immediately. Siswiyono didn't know Pak Karjan had been praying for God to give him an opportunity like this. That weekend Pak Karjan went to his little nest egg of evangelism money, pulled out a few coins, and he and Siswiyono rode the bus to the village of Coconut Mountain where Siswiyono had grown up. That night Siswiyono's family gathered at his folks' home. Pak Karjan sat on the floor and shared with them what he knew about Jesus Christ. When he got to the end, he asked them what they thought. "That was really interesting. Could you come back and tell us more?" came the reply.

Indeed he could. As often as possible, the two men made the trek back and forth to Coconut Mountain. But it didn't take long for Pak Karjan's meager purse of evangelism money to be exhausted. He began to plead with God for help.

It was at this point that he heard about the Church of the Nazarene. I remember well the morning I heard the knock on my door and opened it to the short, older, Indonesian man who greeted me with a large, almost toothless, smile. I admit I invited him in with reluctance. But as he began to tell his story, he gripped my heart. When he got to the end he said, "Missionary, how about it? Could the Church of the Nazarene afford the couple dollars it takes to pay my round-trip bus fare to Coconut Mountain?" I told him we had a wonderful church around the world who had sacrificially given to missions and that I thought we could help him. Thus began a partnership that is still thriving.

Using World Evangelism Fund monies, we began to help pay for Pak Karjan's bus fare. Soon he began a weekly ministry in Coconut Mountain, and the small community of believers started to grow. Before long, it became apparent he could be so much more effective if he was living up there and working full-time. So we rented a building that could double as a home and a church and replaced his salary from the chrome shop with a salary from the World Evangelism Fund. The church grew. Before long it was organized as the first Nazarene church in Central Java.

Not long after that, Pak Karjan met with our District Advisory Board. "God has blessed us in

Coconut Mountain," he said. "When I first went there, there was no one, but now we have a strong church. They need someone better trained to pastor them. I have no education." And then with a twinkle in his eye he added, "Besides, God has called me to be a pioneer. I want to go somewhere where there is no church and start one." After much deliberation, the board agreed and reassigned Pak Karjan to begin a Church of the Nazarene in the city of Pracimantoro, deeper into this South Mountain area of Central Java. As we had no Nazarene work anywhere near that area, he would be doing lonely pioneer evangelism. But he was excited.

That's when I decided to use the $10 gift from a hardworking man in the United States to buy Pak Karjan a pair of shoes. I knew he had worn out many pairs of shoes walking long distances on stony paths to bring the gospel to difficult and remote areas. This seemed like the perfect investment.

At our monthly preacher's meeting, I called Pak Karjan off to the side and explained to him that I had money for a new pair of shoes for him. His eyes lit up. He showed me the worn pair he was wearing. Over the next months, I paid particular attention to Pak Karjan's reports. I felt I had a vested interest in his ministry because of the shoes. Sometimes his reports were exciting as he told of new posts, new converts, and young people called into the ministry.

Sometimes they were sobering as he talked about opposition and persecution. But always they were reports of trust and commitment to the task. In the course of Pak Karjan's ministry with the Church of the Nazarene, he has been called before the police 17 different times. He is well past retirement age, but he is still working hard. Through his ministry, we have baptized close to 70 new believers. Two-thirds of our initial class of Bible school graduates came out of his ministry. He is starting his 10th Nazarene church. And the cycle is continuing. He and his wife have five children—three boys and two girls. Four of these young people graduated from INTC. One of the boys started a church north of Yogya. Another is a Christian lay pastor in the factory where he works. Still another is married to a member of the ministry staff of our largest and strongest church in Indonesia. And the fourth child is pastoring the fastest-growing Nazarene church in his zone.

I don't know the name of that man who gave me the $10 bill. He doesn't know how I invested it. But one day he will know, and I have to believe he will feel it is probably the best investment he made in his life. "As it is written, 'How beautiful are the feet of those who bring good news!'" (Rom. 10:15b).

Missions Update

The Church of the Nazarene has 3 organized and 2 pioneer districts in the country of Indonesia. In these 5 areas, we have a total of 52 churches and an additional 61 preaching points that are somewhere in the process of maturing into churches.

"But just as you excel in everything . . . see that you also excel in this grace of giving" (2 Cor. 8:7).

Juanito and Hannah
PHILIPPINES

A number of years ago, a young Filipina named Delia was invited to visit her cousin in Angeles City near a large American air force base. In time, Delia met a military friend of her cousin. They fell in love, married, and moved to a new assignment in Alexandria, Louisiana. Through the invitation of Nazarene friends, Delia began attending a local Nazarene church where she accepted the Lord as her Savior. Delia had not been saved long when she began to think about her sister, Lorna, back in the Philippines. Delia prayed her sister would also find the Lord. In fact, it became such a great concern to her that she wrote a letter to the mission director in the Philippines. She asked if someone would contact Lorna, who was living in the fishing village of Pulapandan on the Island of Negros, to tell her about Jesus.

A team was sent from the Nazarene school in the nearby town of Iloilo to make the initial contact. This meant boarding a ferry for the two-hour ride to Negros, then traveling on to the village of Pulapandan to contact Lorna. After disembarking from the ferry, the team walked the long pier that jutted out into the China Sea and began asking around about Lorna Penella. Finally they found someone who knew her and received directions to her house. They went to the house, knocked on the door, and were greeted by Lorna. After introductions, they explained why they were there. She was so thankful someone from the Church of the Nazarene had come and was happy to think her sister in America had been concerned about her. She welcomed her guests into her little *nepa* hut (a house made of thatch and bamboo). They visited with her until it was time for the ferry to return to Iloilo. Before going, however, they asked if the Church of the Nazarene could send someone to hold a Bible study in her home. She was delighted. Working with the Bible school, we began ministry in Pulapandan on a rotational basis sharing ministry assignments between Bible school students, nearby pastors, and missionaries.

From the beginning, God blessed this new church plant in a remarkable way. Lorna faithfully invited her friends, and interest was so high that the district superintendent wrote me [Bob Sr.] and requested I hold an evangelistic campaign in this small village. I was excited about the opportunity. Using an accordion for music, a flip chart for our corporate songbook, a lantern for light, and a bamboo pole across the front for an altar, we were ready to go. God blessed every service. The bamboo-pole altar was lined each night with people seeking the Lord. In fact, so many turned to the Lord that the district superintendent decided to organize a church during the evangelistic campaign. He began visiting in the homes of these new converts to ask if they would be interested in joining the brand-new Church of the Nazarene. Twenty to 30 of these new Christians said they wanted to join. At the end of the final service of the campaign, we asked who would like to become a member of the Pulapandan Church of the Nazarene. We expected about 20 or 30. But 150 people who had been at the altar during those days stepped out and came forward to join the church. We could hardy believe our eyes. The superintendent read the membership section from the Church of the Nazarene *Manual,* and we took them in as charter members.

We then had a problem—150 members, but no building and no pastor. We returned to the Bible school in Iloilo and looked over the roster of students to see who we might assign there. The names of Juanito and Hannah, who were about to graduate, stood out. We called them in to talk with them and began by asking them what they wanted to do when they graduated. "We want to pastor a church," they said.

Juanito and Hannah with their family

We replied, "How about Pulapandan? We have 150 brand-new members who need a pastor. We don't have a building yet, but God will provide."

They thought this would be a good challenge and agreed to take the church. Again we boarded the ferry to Pulapandan, this time to look for a house large enough to accommodate 150 people. We found one. It was a house on stilts measuring about 20 square feet. By western-world standards this was a rather small house, but by Filipino standards the size was more than adequate. We cleaned out the upstairs for Juanito and Hannah to live in and readied the shaded area underneath to use for a church and Sunday School. Soon the young couple moved in and began pastoring. It wasn't long until I received a letter from them saying the house was much too small for the people. They wondered if we could help build a church. I wrote back and told them we had no money at that time to help build a church or buy land. But I assured them we would be praying with them and that the Lord would provide. Not much later we received a monetary gift to buy land for a church, and we chose Pulapandan.

Pastor Juanito began searching up and down the village and soon found a piece of land that seemed adequate. It was narrow but long, reaching right down into the China Sea. And the price was exactly the same as the amount of money we had.

We paid the money and put up a big sign that read, "Future home of the Church of the Nazarene." It wasn't long before I received another letter from the pastor saying, "Our house church is getting smaller all the time. We have the land, but can you help us build our church?" I wrote back saying there was no more money. It was all used up in the land purchase, but God would provide.

While we didn't have money to help with building a church, we did have one valuable tool we frequently loaned out to new church plants: a cement block machine. Well, it's not exactly a "machine." It's actually a block form with a handle on each side. To use it, you also need an old tree stump. First you fill the form with a mixture of sand, cement, and water. Then, to compact the mixture and form the blocks, you thump it hard several times on the tree stump (this is the "machine" part of the operation). We loaned Juanito the block machine, and he was so delighted that on his way home he bought a bag of cement and carried everything out to the project site. He mixed the cement with sand, put it in the form, thumped it down several times, and turned it out on a board he had prepared to hold the drying block. At this point he learned a valuable lesson: salty sand does not mix well with cement. Since he was using ocean sand, it just crumbled. But Pastor Juanito was not easily discouraged. As he was out

The Pulapandan church

calling on his people one day, he saw an old 55-gallon barrel in a neighbor's yard—probably left over from World War II. He asked the man if he could borrow the barrel to use in building his church. He planned to use it to wash the salt out of the sand. The man readily agreed, so Pastor Juanito took the barrel to the project site. Using buckets and pans, he and other church members filled the barrel with water. Then they scooped up the salty sand, washed it clean, and dumped it out on the ground. When the pile got big enough to consume a bag of cement, they made a batch of 40 blocks. They kept up this process until they had enough blocks to build their church. The hole in the sand got a bit deep, but they had their blocks.

Now that the cement blocks were made, they began to look for rock for the foundation and wall posts. But it seemed there were no rocks at all in that China Sea village—only sand. They wrote me another letter: "Brother McCroskey, we have finished making our blocks, but now we need rock and there is none. It will be very expensive to truck the rock in from outside our area. Could you please help us buy rock?" Again I had to write back and say the money was gone, but I told them we would pray for God to provide.

Forty years before we ever set foot in Pulapandan, God was stockpiling the rock we would need.

We had no way of knowing this at that time, but four decades earlier God was already making provisions for this church. During World War II, United States servicemen joined together with Filipinos to fight for freedom. The American military needed places to safely store supplies and armament, and Pulapandan was the perfect location for such a stockpile. It had a nice big, flat, sandy shore that led right into the ocean. The army loaded barges with crushed rock from quarries in the United States, towed them across the Pacific Ocean, and unloaded them on strategically situated islands throughout the Philippines—including the island of Negros where Pulapandan is located. Unbelievably, some of those barges unloaded the crushed rock from America on the very piece of land God gave for our church. Forty years before we ever set foot in Pulapandan, before we even bought a piece of land for a church or began to form blocks for the building, God was stockpiling the rock we would need.

When the war ended, time and tides completely covered this layer of crushed rock with a deep layer of sand. No one remembered the rock was there. No one but God, that is. One day one of our men working on the project site began to dig on the edge of our property. I do not know why he dug there and why he dug so deep, but suddenly his shovel struck something hard, He brushed away the sand and ran back to the pastor shouting, "We've struck the rock! Pastor, we've struck the rock!"

Trucks came from far and wide to haul off part of this rock. We merely pushed ours up in a wheel barrow and built one of the finest churches in the Philippines. Truly God is a God of miracles, and He has plans for us long before we know our needs.

Jesus told the parable about the foolish builders building on the sand, but the wise builders building on the rock (Matt. 7:24-27). He applied it to the wise person building his life on the teachings of the Eternal Rock of Ages. For the Pulapandan church, this Eternal Rock of Ages even went so far as to provide the physical rock foundation on which the building was constructed as well as the spiritual rock foundation it needed to thrive.

Missions Update

The Church of the Nazarene has 11 organized districts in the Republic of the Philippines. Three of these are mature Phase 3 districts. We have a total of 255 churches and another 50-60 preaching points that have been assisted by our various JESUS film teams. We have more than 18,340 members in these 11 districts.

Epilogue

We have enjoyed telling you these stories as we are all members of the same spiritual family of faith. Family members count on other family members for help, support, and encouragement. We hope our stories will strengthen your faith just as your assistance has strengthened ours.

Thanks to each of you for the times you have given to missions down through the years. Maybe it was a few pennies or a nickel or dime sealed up in a small offering envelope and given to a visiting missionary or placed in an offering plate. Maybe it was a final $10 dollar bill you couldn't afford to give, but couldn't afford not to give. Maybe it was a $5 gift for radio ministry or toward a Faith Promise budget. Or maybe it was money to buy land and build a church like the one in Pulapandan.

We are also thankful to God for the effective evangelism tools He has provided for us to use: tents, boats, motorcycles, bicycles, television, and even radio. More recently we have used the *JESUS* film. What an impact it has made in the lives of so many people.

Thank you also for telling the story of Jesus that changes so many lives. For Pepi, it was a missionary who came to his village. For James, it was an unknown pastor passing through town. You never know the impact of your witness on someone else's life. We want you to know that just as you tell the story of God to others, they are sharing the story with people whose hearts are also being transformed by the indwelling Lord of love.

Above all, thank you for praying without ceasing. In all of our stories, you have seen the unusual timing of events. A visiting pastor prayed and felt led to witness to a young receptionist, and James found God. Prayer led Pepi to begin a Sunday School class within listening distance of a paralyzed lady so God could change her life, her children's lives, and her grandchildren's lives. A truck crank that snapped back led to lost teeth, and a found life. And only God could have orchestrated the events leading to buried rock, purchased land, and an old man doggedly digging deep with his shovel to find the rock. We prayed, you prayed, and God had the answer just waiting to be dug up.

We feel a nudge in our side again to say thanks on behalf of our people in Indonesia and the Philippines. Thank you for giving, going, and witnessing. Thank you for bringing the gospel to them. They, in turn, now know they are debtors to share the hope of the gospel in the same measure they have received it.

Call to Action

After reading this book, consider doing one or more of the following:

1. Pray for the individuals whose stories are told in this book. Ask God to continue to guide them in their ministries and watch over their families.
2. Pray for God to open doors for new work in unreached areas of Indonesia and the Philippines.
3. Pray for the faculty, students, and staff of the Nazarene higher education institutions throughout Asia.
4. Participate in Faith Promise events and offerings, knowing your support provides effective ministry tools for missionaries around the world.
5. Check out how the Church of the Nazarene is effectively using media, including radio, to reach the people of the Asia-Pacific region. Log onto their web site at <www.wmc-ap.org>.
6. Thank God for generations of families like the McCroskeys who follow God's leading into missionary service. Ask God to raise up new workers to follow in their steps.

Aimee Curtis, editor

Pronunciation Guide

The following information will assist in pronouncing some unfamiliar words in this book. The suggested pronunciations, though not always precise, are close approximations of the way the terms are pronounced.

Introduction
Yogyakarta   johg-juh-KAHR-tah

Chapter 1
Acy Lodja   AHCH-ee LOH-jah
Bali   BAH-li
Becak   BE-chahk
Biak   BEE-ahk
Insan Brasi   EEN-sahn BRAH-zi
Irian Jaya   eer-ee-en JIE-ah
Jayapura   jie-ya-PEW-rah
Kalimantan   kah-lee-MAHN-tahn
Papua   pah-PUH-ah
Semarang   se-MAH-rahng
Sumatra   suh-MAH-trah
Yohan   JOH-hahn

Chapter 2
Bajoyo   bah-HOY-oh
Barangays   BAH-ren-giez
De la Peret   day lah puh-RAY
Iloilo   EE-loh EE-loh

Leyte	LAY-tee
Luzon	lew-ZAWN
Mansunsun	mahn-SOON-soon
Mindanao	min-duh-NOU
Mongorocoro	mahng-goh-ROH-koh-roh
Nacionales	na-see-oh-NAH-lays
Negros	NE-grohs
Palawan	puh-LA-wahn
Panay	puh-NIE
Pattee	pa-TEE
Samar	SAH-mahr
Sinot	SEE-noht

Chapter 3

Ambarawa	ahm-bah-RAH-wah
Kicik-kicik	KEE-cheek
Kyai	KEE-yie
Rupiah	REW-pee-yah
Sukarli	su-KAHR-lee
Yez	YEZ

Chapter 4

Bustamante	bew-stah-MAHN-tee
Moncada	mohn-KAHD-ah
Paniqui	pahn-EE-kee
Tolega	toh-LAY-ga

Chapter 5

Gendurit	gen-DEW-rit
Kernet	KER-net
Magelang	MAH-ge-lahng
Pak Karjan	PAHK KAHR-jahn
Pracimantoro	prah-chee-mahn-TOH-roh

Siswiyono   sis-wee-YOH-noh

Chapter 6
Angeles   AHNG-guh-lees
Lorna Penella   LOHR-nah pe-NAY-lah
Nepa   NEE-puh
Pulapandan   pew-lah-PAHN-dahn